A HISTORICAL ALBUM OF

TEXAS

A HISTORICAL ALBUM OF
TEXAS

Charles A. Wills

THE MILLBROOK PRESS, Brookfield, Connecticut

Front and back cover: "East side Main Plaza, San Antonio, Texas," painting by William G. M. Samuel, 1849. Courtesy of the San Antonio Museum Association.

Title page: Big Bend National Park. Courtesy of the Texas Department of Transportation, Travel, and Information Division, Austin, Texas.

Library of Congress Cataloging-in-Publication Data

Wills, Charles.
    A historical album of Texas / Charles A. Wills.
       p. cm. — (Historical albums)
    Includes bibliographical references and index.
    Summary: A history of Texas, from its early exploration and settlement
to the state today.
    ISBN 1-56294-504-1 (lib. bdg.) ISBN 1-56294-847-4 (pbk.)
    1. Texas—History—Juvenile literature. 2. Texas—Gazetteers—
Juvenile literature. I. Title. II. Series.
F386.3.W55 1995
976.4—dc20   94-37395
                                                CIP
                                                AC

Created in association with **Media Projects Incorporated**

    C. Carter Smith, *Executive Editor*
    Lelia Wardwell, *Managing Editor*
    Charles A. Wills, *Principal Writer*
    Bernard Schleifer, *Art Director*
    Shelley Latham, *Production Editor*
    Arlene Goldberg, *Cartographer*

Consultant: John M. Arévalo, Social Studies teacher, Harlandale High School, San Antonio, Texas.

CONTENTS

Introduction

Texas stands out from the other American states because of its sheer size and the awesome variety of its landscape. Stretching 800 miles from north to south and almost as far from east to west, Texas is a giant; until Alaska joined the Union in 1959, Texas was by far the largest state. Within its 262,000 square miles can be found pine forests and gently rolling coastal lowlands; vast stretches of treeless plains; rugged mountains and sunbaked near-desert (a landscape of rock, sand, and dry grasslands).

But impressive as it is, Texas's size is more than matched by its long and lively history. First colonized by Spain (with competition from France) three centuries ago, then ruled by Mexico, the land once known as Tejas attracted American settlers in the 1820s and 1830s. It wasn't long before these rugged newcomers broke away from Mexico, and for almost a decade the Republic of Texas was an independent nation.

This independent spirit lives on today. Texans of all kinds see themselves as tough, proud, self-reliant people—and they usually are. An example: In 1989, Texas's highway commission decided that license plates would bear the slogan "The Friendship State." Although the decision met with a storm of protest, the slogan remained the same. Ann Richards, a governor of the state, summed up the reaction of many Texans when she said of the slogan: "It's wimpy."

In the century and a half since Texas became a part of the United States, the state has known boom and bust, triumph and tragedy. It has seen the rapid growth of many important industries, from cattle raising to oil. Its major cities—Dallas and Houston particularly—are among the biggest and most prosperous urban centers in the West. Always a bit larger than life, Texas remains a giant among the states.

PART ONE

FROM COLONY TO REPUBLIC

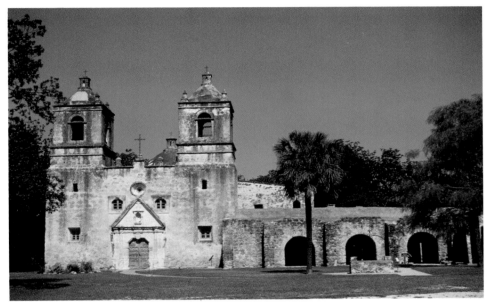

The Spanish mission was the place where most of Texas's Native Americans first encountered Europeans. Mission Concepción, above, dates back to the 1600s.

The saga of Texas begins with the Native American peoples. In the 15th century Spain became the first of six nations to claim Texas. France was the second, although only briefly. By the time Mexico's flag was raised over Texas, Americans had begun to settle there in large numbers. In 1835, these settlers revolted against the Mexican government, finally securing their independence with a brilliant victory at the Battle of San Jacinto. After ten years as an independent country, Texas became the twenty-eighth state of the Union, sparking the Mexican War. The United States won, but soon Texas was at war again, this time as part of the Confederacy fighting against the North.

The First Texans

Human beings have lived in Texas for tens of thousands of years. In the distant past, a land bridge connected the continents of Asia and North America. Across this bridge came the first humans to North America—the people scholars call Paleo-Americans. Over many centuries, these people spread throughout the continent, finally reaching the vast region that is today the state of Texas.

Texas at this time was a very different place from what it is now. Much of the land was covered with grass and trees. Over the centuries, the land became hotter, drier, and less hospitable to early humans. Eventually, the Paleo-American Culture died out.

About 7,000 years ago, new groups began arriving in Texas from the north. These peoples, known as Neo-Americans ("New Americans") or, simply, Native Americans, developed distinctive cultures in Texas's varied landscape.

The largest Native American group in Texas was the Caddos, a nation of more than twenty-four separate tribes that lived in the pine forests to the east. The Caddos were also the most advanced of the Texas peoples; some anthropologists believe they were related to the great Indian civilizations of Mexico and Central America, and to the mound-building societies of the Mississippi River Valley.

Because they lived in a region with plentiful rainfall and good soil, the Caddos lived by farming as well as by hunting. They raised crops of corn and vegetables and they lived in large houses of wood topped with roofs of grass thatching. They were also skilled in the arts of pottery, woodcarving, and weaving. Caddo society was highly organized, with a ruling class and a priesthood to oversee each village's political and religious life. The Caddos traded with the peoples who lived on the plains to the west, exchanging cloth, wooden tools, and weapons for buffalo hides.

South of the Caddos lived the Arkokisas, the Attacapas, the Bidais, the Deadoses, and the Karankawas. Their homeland was the hot, humid coast of the Gulf of Mexico where life was a constant struggle for survival. Gulf tribes never became as sophisticated as the Caddos.

The Coahuiltecans lived on the dry grasslands to the west. They ate wild plants like the root of the agave plant and the beans of the mesquite bush.

To the north, on the edge of the Great Plains, were the Tonkawans. They depended on the buffalo for food, shelter, clothing, and tools.

The last Native American group to arrive in Texas before the coming of the Europeans was the Apaches. A fierce, warlike people, the Apaches defeated other Indian groups in their constant quest for new hunting grounds.

This early 19th-century painting (above) shows a peaceful encampment of a Lipan Apache band. The Lipans were settled in western Texas and were closely related to some Mexican tribes. An Apache band consisted of several extended families and one appointed leader.

The Native American nations that lived on the plains of western Texas spoke a variety of languages. To communicate, the different Indian groups relied on sign language. In this engraving (right), an Apache makes the sign for "winter."

Conquistadors and Comanches

At the end of the 15th century, Spanish navigators reached the Caribbean Islands and the continents of North and South America—lands they called "the New World." The navigators were followed by *conquistadors*, or conquerors, determined to win land for Spain and gold and glory for themselves. Together with missionaries who wanted to convert the New World's native peoples to the Roman Catholic Church, the conquistadors claimed much land in the Americas—including present-day Texas—for the Spanish crown.

The first European to reach Texas was probably Alonso Álvarez de Piñeda, a Spanish sea captain. In 1519, the same year Hernan Cortés conquered the Aztec Empire in what is now called Mexico, Álvarez sailed along the Gulf Coast, possibly reaching the mouth of the Rio Grande.

Nine years later, a large Spanish *entrada* (expedition) under the command of Panfilo de Narváez left Mexico to explore the region to the north. When the expedition's ships were wrecked on the Florida coast, some of the explorers tried to return to Mexico in crude boats. Four men —Alvar Núñez Cabeza de Vaca, two companions, and an African slave named Estavanico—were again shipwrecked, this time on the Texas coast.

For the next eight years, the four men journeyed throughout Texas and the Southwest. For much of that time, the castaways were prisoners of various Native American groups. They finally reached the safety of a Spanish outpost in northern Mexico.

During their captivity in Texas, Cabeza de Vaca and his companions heard tales of great cities of gold in the Southwest. These stories inspired the Spanish to send an army of soldiers and Catholic missionaries led by Francisco Vásquez de Coronado in search of the cities. Marching from Mexico in 1541, Coronado passed through Texas and traveled as far north as present-day Kansas. But Coronado didn't find any gold.

In 1598, another great entrada commanded by Juan de Oñate, governor of New Mexico, crossed the Rio Grande and formally claimed Texas for Spain. More than eighty years passed, however, before Spain planted a colony in Texas: Ysleta, a small settlement near present-day El Paso, was established in 1682.

In the 17th century the flag of France appeared in Texas. In 1685, French explorer Robert Cavalier, Sieur de La Salle, led an expedition to the mouth of the Mississippi River. La Salle's ships went off course and landed instead in Texas at Matagorda Bay.

The Frenchmen built an outpost, Fort St. Louis, while La Salle journeyed in search of the Mississippi. On one of these trips, La Salle was killed.

Word of the French settlement reached the Spanish to the south. Not wanting to see Texas settled by a rival nation, authorities in Mexico sent an expedition against Fort St. Louis. The Spanish soldiers found only ruins in 1689.

In the late 1600s and early 1700s, the Spanish built several missions (religious settlements) and *presidios* (forts) in Texas. The most important

In a modern artist's reconstruction, Cabeza de Vaca and his three companions gaze out over the rugged, sun-drenched landscape of the Southwest. Cabeza de Vaca's account of his journey, *La Relación*, published in 1542, helped spark Spanish interest in exploring and colonizing the region of Texas.

of these early settlements was San Antonio de Bexar, founded in 1718 on the site of the future city of San Antonio. Most of the settlers were *mestizos*—people of mixed Spanish and Native American ancestry brought north from Mexico.

The Spanish were not the only new arrivals in the region during these years. A new Native American group, the Comanches, appeared in Texas. A buffalo-hunting people of the Great Plains, the Comanches had obtained horses by raiding Spanish settlements in New Mexico. Excellent riders and fierce fighters, the Comanches soon spread into Texas. The coming of the Comanches had an effect on Texas's native peoples. The Comanches pushed the Apaches from their lands. The Apaches in turn overran the Coahuiltecans and other groups.

With warfare raging on the Texas frontier, Spanish settlement slowed. By the last decade of the 18th century, only about 4,000 colonists, including 1,000 soldiers, lived in Texas.

Mounted on swift horses and bearing lances, these Comanche warriors are shown riding into battle. The Comanches fought an on-going war against Spanish, Mexican, and finally American settlement that lasted for hundreds of years.

"Gone to Texas"

By the late 1700s, Texas had a new neighbor to the north—the United States. The Louisiana Purchase of 1803, doubling the size of the young country, put America on Texas's doorstep. Until 1819, there was no agreed-upon border between Spanish Texas and United States territory, so the land along the Sabine and Red rivers became a lawless "no-man's land."

Spanish authority was growing weak not only in Texas, but throughout Mexico. A revolt against Spain broke out in 1810. Weakened by war in Europe, Spain couldn't hold onto its North American empire. By 1821 Mexico had achieved independence and gained control of Texas.

Adventurers from the United States had explored the region beginning in the late 1700s and there were a few Americans living in Texas as early as 1803. Then, in 1820, the last year of Spanish rule, a Missouri business-man named Moses Austin arrived in San Antonio. Austin asked for land and permission to settle a number of American families in Texas. The Spanish authorities agreed, but Moses Austin died not long after returning to the United States. The following year, his son, Stephen Austin, led 300 families—now famous as the "Old Three Hundred"—to the banks of the Colorado and Brazos rivers. The American settlement of Texas had begun.

Stephen Austin (below) was not yet thirty years old when he led the first group of Americans to settle along the Brazos River in 1822. Born in Virginia, educated at schools in Connecticut and Kentucky, Austin was a banker and a judge before he took over his father's coloniz-ing efforts in Texas.

When news of Mexican independence reached the small American colony, Austin journeyed to Mexico City to persuade the new government to allow the American Texans to remain. Hoping that American settlers would make their long-neglected colony prosperous, the Mexican authorities confirmed Austin's land grant, as long as the Americans accepted Mexican citizenship and the Roman Catholic religion. Other Americans also received land grants under the same terms.

Lured by free or cheap land in Texas, thousands of settlers, most of them from the South, headed to small Texas towns like Washington-on-the-Brazos. The letters "GTT"—"gone to Texas"—began to appear on the doors of abandoned cabins throughout the Mississippi Valley. Between 1820 and 1835, some 25,000 Americans arrived in Texas. About one in every five of these newcomers was an African-American slave. (Slavery was illegal in Mexico, but the Mexican government allowed the practice in Texas.)

As far as the Mexican government was concerned, the American settlement of Texas proved almost too successful. Instead of becoming a prosperous province of Mexico, Texas began to look like an American outpost in Mexican territory.

The American Texans traded freely with the United States, but such trade brought few economic benefits to Mexico. And despite their pledges to

General Antonio López de Santa Anna (above) was elected president of Mexico in 1833 and two years later became dictator. He made it clear to the Mexican government that he would not give the Texans their independence.

become Mexican citizens and Roman Catholics, American Texans often disobeyed Mexican laws and kept their Protestant religion. There was little the Mexican government, far away in Mexico City, could do to enforce its authority. In 1830, Mexico stopped granting land to American colonizers and banned further American settlement in Texas.

For their part, the American Texans grew more and more dissatisfied with Mexican rule, especially after General Antonio López de Santa Anna came to power in 1833. Santa Anna ruled as a dictator, and he had little patience for the American Texans' wishes for more self-government.

"Remember the Alamo!"

At first, Texan leaders such as Stephen Austin pressed the Mexican government for political reforms, not outright independence for Texas. In late 1832 and early 1833, prominent Texans met and drafted petitions calling for the organization of Texas as a Mexican state and a lifting of the ban on American immigration. Austin traveled to Mexico City to present the petitions to the Mexican government.

On his way back to Texas, however, Austin was arrested and thrown in jail. Released in July 1835, Austin decided the time for a peaceful settlement was past. Texans would have to fight for their rights. "War," Austin said, "is our only resource."

The Texan Revolution began on October 2, 1835, when Mexican troops led by General Martín Perfecto de Cós arrived at the village of Gonzales on the Guadalupe River. Cós demanded the return of a small cannon loaned to the Texans years before. The defiant Texans hung a sign on the cannon: COME AND TAKE IT. The Mexican soldiers tried, but they were beaten back and forced to take refuge in San Antonio.

In December, a small Texas force captured San Antonio and forced Cós to surrender. Instead of preparing for a Mexican counterattack, however, many Texan volunteers left San Antonio in an attempt to capture the Mexican town of Matamoros.

When a 5,000-man Mexican army—commanded by Santa Anna himself—arrived at San Antonio on February 23, 1836, only about 190 Texans remained inside the city. Commanded by Lieutenant Colonel William Barrett Travis, the tiny force included many volunteers who had come from the United States, and even overseas, to help the Texans fight for freedom. Among them were two legendary frontiersmen: Davy Crockett of Tennessee, and Jim Bowie of Arkansas, for whom the famous fighting knife is named. The defenders holed up inside the fortified walls of the Alamo, an old mission church.

Santa Anna's troops began their assault before dawn on March 6. Fighting furiously, the Texans killed some 1,500 attackers, but the Alamo's defenders were hopelessly outnumbered. After ninety minutes of savage combat, all the Texans, including a number of *Tejanos* (non-anglos), lay dead or dying.

While Santa Anna prepared his attack, fifty-nine Texan leaders met at Washington-on-the-Brazos for a "Texan Constitutional Convention." On March 3, the delegates approved a Declaration of Independence and appointed David Burnet as the provi-

sional (temporary) president of the Republic of Texas. The war against Santa Anna was now officially a fight for Texan independence.

Not long after the fall of the Alamo, however, the Texans suffered another disaster. While retreating from the town of Goliad, Colonel James Fannin surrendered his 400 men to Mexican general Jose Urrea on March 23. Four days later, the Texan prisoners were lined up and shot.

By now, command of the Texan forces passed to Sam Houston, a forty-two-year-old lawyer with a colorful past. Before coming to Texas in 1832, Houston had lived for years with the Cherokees in Tennessee, fought with General Andrew Jackson, and served as governor of Tennessee. For six weeks, Sam Houston retreated before

Santa Anna's army, trading space for time while building up the Texan volunteers into a force of 1,600 men, including many Tejanos. Finally, Houston's scouts found Santa Anna's army camped along the San Jacinto River.

Shouting "Remember the Alamo!" the Texans swept into Santa Anna's camp on April 21. Within twenty minutes the Mexicans were in retreat, pursued by the Texans, who killed hundreds in revenge for their earlier defeats. Only eight Texans died and twenty-three were wounded, including Houston, who was shot in the leg. About 600 Mexicans died, and 600 more were taken prisoner. The next day, Santa Anna himself was captured.

After the Battle of San Jacinto, Santa Anna tried to escape from the battlefield in a private's uniform, but he was recognized, captured, and brought before the wounded Sam Houston—a scene portrayed in this 1886 painting by William Huddle. The man on the right with his hand to his ear is "Deaf" Smith, the Texan army's chief scout.

The Lone Star Republic

Sam Houston's victory made the words of Texas's Declaration of Independence a reality. A new nation had been born on the battlefield along the San Jacinto River: the Republic of Texas.

Texans of Mexican descent, as well as American Texans, helped build this new nation. The region contained many Mexican Texans who had opposed Santa Anna's dictatorship and fought alongside the "Texians," as the American settlers called themselves. Among them was Jose Antonio Navarro, who helped write Texas's Declaration of Independence. Another was Lorenzo de Zavala, once a high-ranking Mexican politician, who served as the republic's provisional vice president during the first months of independence.

But three quarters of the new nation's citizens were American, and almost all of them wanted Texas to become part of the United States. Unfortunately, the great political issue of the time—slavery—stood in the way. If Texas was admitted to the

Union as a slave state, it would upset the delicate political balance in Congress between the Northern (free) and Southern (slave) states.

Thus, many Northern politicians fought efforts to annex Texas—that is, to declare it part of the United States. America officially recognized the Republic of Texas as a nation in 1837, but the following year an annexation proposal failed to clear the House of Representatives.

In the meantime, the Texans set about organizing the government of their new nation. Elections to fill the government posts were held in September 1836. Sam Houston won the presidency in a landslide, and Mirabeau Lamar became vice president. Stephen Austin won election as the republic's first secretary of state, but he died soon after taking office.

This woodcut (above) shows Austin, capital of the Republic of Texas, in about 1840. At the time, fewer than a thousand people lived in this rugged frontier town on the Colorado River. The large house on the hill belonged to Mirabeau Lamar, who became the republic's president in 1838.

Much of the culture and architecture in southern Texas reflects a strong Mexican influence (25 percent of the population in the republic was of Mexican descent by 1936). This painting (opposite) shows a Mexican funeral procession through the streets of San Antonio.

In 1839, the tiny settlement of Waterloo was chosen as Texas's capital and renamed in Austin's honor. That same year, Texas adopted a national flag. Its design was simple—a single white star on a blue background, with a red and a white stripe.

At times, people wondered how long this lone star flag would wave over an independent Texas. Despite the Texan victory at San Jacinto, Mexico would not accept the loss of its former territory.

Before returning to Mexico, Santa Anna had signed a peace treaty recognizing Texan independence, but the Mexican government refused to confirm the agreement. Throughout its ten-year existence, the republic was the scene of occasional battles between armed Texan settlers and Mexican soldiers.

In these conflicts, Mexico scored some successes—San Antonio, for example, was briefly recaptured in 1842—but Texas preserved its independence. Much of the credit goes to Texas's navy, which kept its ports on the Gulf of Mexico open and sometimes raided Mexican coastal towns.

While Mexico made efforts to reclaim Texas, there were many Texans who wanted to enlarge their republic by taking land from Mexico. Several expeditions—some of which were backed by the Texas government—ventured into Mexican territory to seize land and set up "colonies," but none was successful.

The new nation also fought many long-running conflicts with Native Americans. In East Texas, a new Indian nation had appeared on the scene—the Cherokees. Driven from their homeland in the southeastern states by white settlement, the Cher-okees wanted to farm in peace. President Houston, an old friend of the Cherokee nation, honored their land claims. When Mirabeau Lamar succeeded Houston as president in 1838, however, he forced most of the Cherokees out of the republic.

Farther west, there was bitter, bloody fighting with the Comanches as settlers moved onto their tribal lands. The war with the Comanches reached its climax in the early 1840s, when peace talks failed and Comanche war parties cut a trail of death and destruction all the way to the Gulf of Mexico. Years of skirmishing followed, with suffering on both sides. The story was much the same with other Native American nations on the Texas frontier.

The Lone Star Republic had other worries besides tense relations with Mexico and constant conflict with the Native Americans. Texas had almost no roads and few large towns. The government started out with no money in its treasury, and economic problems plagued the republic all through its brief life.

But Texas did have one thing to offer—plenty of land. So much land, in fact, that the government gave it away: Any family arriving in Texas could apply to receive a grant of 1,280 acres. A single settler got half that amount. As in the *empresario* days—when colonization of the territory was actively promoted—before the Texan Revolution, the lure of

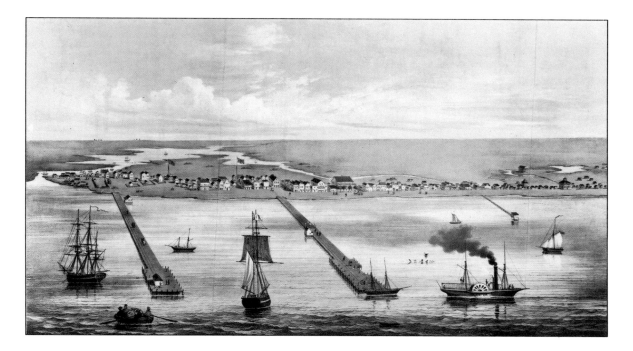

land brought thousands of settlers to Texas. Between 1836 and 1846, Texas's population rose from less than 40,000 to 140,000.

Settlement in Texas followed a regional pattern. The wooded land of north Texas became home to many small farmers. The flat, humid strip of land along the Gulf Coast and the river valleys of east Texas proved ideal for growing cotton and sugar, and newcomers established large plantations, often worked by slaves. The Gulf ports grew prosperous from trade with the United States—for many years, Galveston was Texas's most important city, although San Antonio remained the largest Texas town until after the Civil War. And as the Comanches were forced back and west

The Gulf Coast town of Indianola, shown here as it looked in the 1840s, was the port of entry for many immigrants to Texas from Europe. Hurricanes in 1875 and 1886 led to the town's abandonment. Today, all that remains of the once-thriving port is a historical marker.

Texas opened to new settlement, cattle ranches began to spring up across the plains.

Attracted by the prospect of land and freedom in the new nation, immigrants from overseas joined the flood of Americans eager to try their luck in Texas. Thousands of people from Ireland, Britain, Scandinavia, and Central Europe arrived in Texas in the late 1830s and 1840s. The biggest immigrant group came from Germany. A

"Society for the Protection of German Immigrants in Texas" was set up in Germany in the early 1840s, and the organization brought thousands of Germans to central Texas, where the newcomers built the towns of New Braunfels, Castell, and Fredericksburg. The German settlers got along remarkably well with the Native Americans: Their peace treaty with the local Comanches is remembered today as one of the few agreements between whites and Native Americans that was honored by both sides.

This painting shows the 1847 meeting between German settlers led by John Meusebach and Comanches of the Penateka band. In return for $3,000 in gifts, the Comanches agreed to share their land with the newcomers.

Annexation and War

In 1841, Sam Houston succeeded Mirabeau Lamar and began a second term as president of the Republic of Texas. Houston had never given up hope of seeing Texas enter the United States, and in the early 1840s he did his best to achieve this goal.

To force Congress to tackle the issue, the Texas government strengthened diplomatic ties with Great Britain and France. There were hints that if the United States didn't annex Texas, the Lone Star Republic might put itself under the "protection" of a European power. In truth, there was little chance that Texas would do so, but Houston and other leading Texans wanted the American government to take action. They succeeded: In October 1843, negotiations toward an annexation agreement began.

Although slavery still made annexation a risky political issue, many Americans now favored bringing Texas into the Union. In the 1840s, there was growing feeling among Americans that the United States should widen its territory and expand to the Pacific Ocean. (Later, a newspaper editorial would give this idea a name—Manifest Destiny.) Annexing Texas seemed like a natural first step toward this goal.

In the United States, annexation was a major issue in the presidential campaign of 1844. Democratic candidate James K. Polk was an outspoken champion of annexation; Whig nominee Henry Clay, however, refused to commit himself.

Polk's narrow victory in November cleared the way for annexation, but it was the outgoing president, John Tyler, who set the stage. Tyler realized that an annexation treaty might not pass the Senate, where a two-thirds majority was required for approval. Thus, shortly before leaving office, Tyler instead asked Congress to annex Texas by a joint resolution of the House and Senate. The resolution passed on February 28, 1845.

Under the resolution's terms, Texas would be admitted to the Union as a state, skipping the territorial stage most other new states went through. Furthermore, Texas would have the right to split itself into as many as five new states if it so chose. (Technically, Texas can do so even today.)

Texan voters approved the annexation resolution, and on December 29, 1845, President Polk signed the Texas Admission Act into law. The Republic of Texas was now the twenty-eighth state of the Union.

On February 19, 1846, the American flag replaced the Lone Star flag atop the Texas capitol. "The final act of this great drama is upon us," said

Anson Jones, the republic's last president. "The Republic of Texas is no more."

Within months of Texas's admission, the United States and Mexico went to war. The Mexican government had long warned that annexation might result in armed conflict. In addition, the two nations disagreed on the border between Texas and Mexico.

In the spring of 1846, President Polk sent an "Army of Observation" to the disputed border area along the Nueces River and the Rio Grande. A skirmish between American and Mexican forces in May led to sixteen months of war. The fighting ended with a victorious American army capturing Mexico City.

News of the outbreak of war with Mexico reaches a small-town post office in this painting (above, left). Some Americans opposed Texas's annexation on the grounds that it would lead to war with Mexico—which is exactly what happened.

Some 8,000 Texans fought in the Mexican War, including six companies of the famous Texas rangers—a force originally raised by the Republic of Texas to fight Comanches. This painting (left) shows U.S. troops battling their way into Mexico City. Among them was Ulysses S. Grant, then a young captain and later Union commander in the Civil War and president of the United States.

Under the Confederate Flag

The American victory in the Mexican War produced a political dispute between Texas and the federal government. The peace treaty that ended the war set Texas's southern boundary at the Rio Grande, but said nothing about its western border. Texas's government felt the state should extend westward into land won from Mexico, while the federal government wanted to create a new territory, New Mexico, from that land. In 1850, Texas agreed to give up its claim to New Mexico in return for $10 million, and the new state's northern and western borders were established as they are today.

But slavery continued to cast a shadow over Texas, as it did over the entire nation. At this time, most people in the North were willing to accept slavery in the South, but not in the new territories of the West. Southern politicians, meanwhile, opposed any effort to limit slavery. Political compromises attempted to keep the peace between North and South, but as the 1850s wore on, the two sections of the country found it harder and harder to get along.

Texas depended on slavery for its cotton industry, one of the biggest agricultural products for the state. Slaves worked long, hot days in cotton fields gathering the crop, as shown in this illustration.

Texas wasn't part of the South, but it was a slave state, and nine out of every ten Anglo Texans—that is, Texans not of Native American or Mexican ancestry—had roots in the South. Thus, most Texans supported the South as the nation drifted toward civil war.

As senator (1846–49) and governor (1859–61), Sam Houston worked to preserve the Union. "When Texas united her destiny with that of the United States," he said in 1859, "she entered not into the North nor into the South. Her connection was not sectional, but national."

Beginning in December 1860, however, Southern states began to secede (withdraw) from the Union. Texas would have to take sides. In a statewide vote held in February 1861, Texans voted by a margin of about three to one to join the seceded states in the newly formed Confederate States of America. Heartbroken, Sam Houston refused to take an oath of loyalty to the Confederacy and was forced into retirement.

Four years of war between the Union and the Confederacy began in April 1861. Not much fighting would take place in Texas, but the state still played an important role in the war. Between 60,000 and 70,000 Texan men went east to serve in the Confederate Army. (About 2,000 Texans decided to fight for the Union.) The Texas Brigade, a Confederate unit commanded by the legendary John Bell Hood, won fame for hard fighting in many major battles. On the political side, Texan John H. Reagan served as postmaster-general in the Confederate cabinet.

Texas served as a gateway for supplies destined for the Confederacy by way of Mexico. Much of this trade was carried on through the state's Gulf Coast ports. To keep these much needed goods from reaching the South, the Union began blockading Texas's coastal towns. In October 1862, Union forces captured Galveston. In a daring operation on New Year's Day 1863, Confederate forces recaptured the port, and it remained in Confederate hands until the end of the war.

Texan forces also turned back a Union expedition aimed at capturing Sabine Pass, where the Sabine and Neches rivers flow into the Gulf of Mexico. In January 1863, a tiny Texan force of fewer than fifty troops and a handful of cannons kept 5,000 Union troops from landing and capturing the pass. The following year, an even larger Union force tried to invade Texas by way of the Red River, but Confederate forces halted the Union advance at the Texas border.

By the spring of 1865, however, the Confederacy was on its last legs. In April, the fighting ended with Confederate commander Robert E. Lee's surrender at Appomattox, Virginia. Word of the surrender didn't reach far-off Texas until weeks later.

Although bitterly opposed to secession, Sam Houston (right) approved his son's decision to join the Confederate Army: "If Texas demands your services or your life in her cause," he wrote, "stand by her."

Union troops charge Confederate general John Bell Hood's Texans in this scene (below) from the bloody battle of Antietam, fought in Maryland in September 1862. A Kentuckian by birth but a Texan by choice, Hood was a hard fighter, although he proved much too hot-tempered for high command.

In the meantime, the last battle of the Civil War was fought on Texas soil. On May 11, Union and Confederate troops clashed at Palmitto Ranch outside Brownsville. The Southerners won the battle only to discover that they had lost the war.

The end of the Civil War was not the end of conflict in Texas. During the years after the war—the period known as Reconstruction—many white Texans bitterly opposed federal demands to guarantee civil and political rights to the state's newly freed slaves. Violent attacks on African Americans became common. Political infighting made matters worse for all Texans.

After several years under military rule, Texas adopted a new state constitution and was readmitted to the Union in 1870. The hard feelings of the Reconstruction years lingered for a long time. For the state's African Americans, the end of Reconstruction in the 1870s meant the loss of the rights they had gained just a short time before.

Emancipation—freedom—came to Texas's slaves on June 19, 1865. The date has been celebrated by the state's African Americans ever since as "Juneteenth." Unfortunately, slavery in Texas gave way to the hardship, violence, and unfair treatment African Americans suffered under Reconstruction.

PART TWO

THE LONE STAR STATE

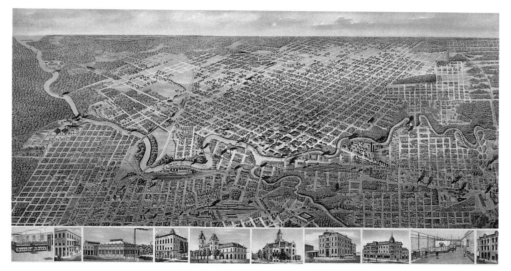

This panoramic lithograph shows Houston at the turn of the 20th century, when it was Texas's second-largest city with a population of about 45,000.

After four years of civil war followed by a painful period of Reconstruction, Texas rejoined the Union. Soon the state began to prosper, thanks to the great cattle drives of the 1870s and 1880s. Oil strikes in the first decades of the 20th century brought wealth, but the state suffered during the Depression of the 1930s. World War II turned Texas into a major industrial state, and, despite economic ups and downs, Texas grew to become the third-largest state in population. In recent decades, Texas's African-American and Hispanic communities have sought a greater share of the state's economic and political life, and Texans of all kinds have been active on the national political scene.

Cowboys and Cattle Drives

Like other ex-Confederate states, Texas might have spent the decades after the Civil War in an economic slump. Instead, Texas was booming again just a few years after the guns fell silent.

The state owed this good fortune to the Spanish explorers, soldiers, and settlers who had colonized Texas centuries before. The Spanish had brought cattle with them from their homeland. Over the years, the descendants of these animals multiplied. By the mid-1860s, between 3 and 4 million head of hardy cattle—soon to be famous as Texas Longhorns—roamed the state's grasslands.

Cattle raising was a long-standing business in Texas. Ranches, or *haciendas*, had been established during the Spanish and Mexican eras. The missions run by the Catholic Church often kept their own herds, some numbering as many as 15,000 head.

In the years before the Civil War, a number of Texans went into the ranching business, most notably Richard King and Mifflin Kennedy, two former riverboat captains. In 1860, King and Kennedy began buying up land, laying the foundation for the great King Ranch, which eventually covered almost 750,000 acres—an area bigger than the entire state of Rhode Island.

The growth of the ranching business on the western plains of Texas brought many more settlers into the area. In response, Kiowa and Comanche raiders increased attacks on settlers during and after the Civil War. In 1864, the U.S. Army fought back against the Comanches in a battle on the Staked Plain of the Texas Panhandle and subsequent campaigns, in an effort to move the tribes onto reservations set up by the U.S. government.

Most Plains Indians were reluctant to leave the open land. They had lived as buffalo hunters for generations and did not want to be forced to change their way of life completely.

An important Indian leader in the fight for the Texas plains was Quanah Parker. The son of a white woman and a Comanche chief, Quanah was a fierce warleader during the final phase of Comanche resistance in Texas in the 1870s. Quanah and other leaders conducted raids on cavalry units and white buffalo hunters in a series of conflicts that came to be known as the Red River War, fought in the Texas Panhandle in 1874–75. The U.S. Army, with its larger forces and superior firearms, had the upper hand. The following June, Quanah Parker and his Comanche warriors surrendered to the army and moved onto a reservation—leaving the plains open for farms and ranches.

The early ranchers kept cattle not for beef, but for hides, which were sold for leather, and for tallow (fat).

In a broad-brimmed hat and leather chaps, a Texas cowboy keeps an eye on his herd. Frederic Remington painted this romantic view (above) in 1904, two decades after the era of the cattle drives had drawn to a close.

Satanta (right), also known as White Bear, was a Kiowa leader who negotiated with government officials for reservation land. He became known as "the Orator of the Plains" for his eloquence in public speaking. "I love the land and buffalo, and will not part with it," he said in a speech. "A long time ago this land belonged to our fathers; but when I go up the river I see camps of soldiers . . . [who] cut down my timber; they kill my buffalo, and when I see that, my heart feels like bursting."

Raising cattle for meat didn't become profitable until after the Civil War, when an increased demand for beef arose in the Northern states. A steer could be bought for $4 in Texas in 1866; in Chicago, the same animal sold for $40.

Texas had plenty of cattle to meet the rising demand. The problem was how to get the animals from Texas to the Kansas Pacific railroad, which extended only as far south as Abilene, Kansas. From there, the animals could be shipped to the cities for slaughter.

The solution was simply to drive herds of longhorns north to the railroad across the open, unfenced plains. In 1867, the first herd of longhorns went north from the Rio Grande Valley to Abilene along a trail laid out by Jesse Chisholm, a Cherokee.

The Chisholm Trail began the era of the cattle drives, a time of great wealth for Texas and the source of many of the legends of the Wild West. The Chisholm Trail was joined by other trails that ended at rowdy railroad towns like Dodge City in Kansas and Denison in Texas itself. Between 1870 and 1890, about 10 million head of cattle—as many as 700,000 in one year—were driven north.

The men responsible for moving the animals north were, of course, the cowboys. Books, songs, movies, and television have all glorified the life of the cowboy, but the reality differed greatly from the show business version. For one thing, at least one in four cowboys was of African-American or of Mexican ancestry. And the work was difficult and often dangerous.

Driving a herd of 2,000 or so long-horns several thousand miles was an exhausting job for the ten to fifteen cowboys who made up a typical "trail outfit." Cowboys usually spent eighteen or nineteen hours a day in the saddle, enduring the searing Texas heat and the clouds of dust thrown up by the herd. The cowboy's worries didn't end at nightfall; a sudden noise might stampede the herd, scattering thousands of animals across the plains.

The cattle drives could last only as long as the plains were open range-land, and by the 1880s, the open-range era was drawing to a close. By the end of the 19th century, farmers as well as ranchers were using the plains. Farmers didn't want thousands of cattle tramping across their fields, so they began fencing in their land.

Cattleman Henry "Paint" Campbell stands outside a cabin on the outskirts of his ranch in this photograph (opposite).

African-American "cowpunchers" pose outside the town of Bonham, Texas, in this photograph (above). Many African-American cowboys were ex-slaves who went west at the end of the Civil War.

The introduction of barbed wire in 1870 quickened the pace. Soon the ranchers, too, were fencing in their acreage instead of allowing their cattle to graze freely.

What finally ended the great cattle drives was the expansion of the rail-roads into Texas. By 1886, the state had 8,000 miles of track, connecting it to the rest of the country. There was no longer a need for cowboys to

drive the herds north to meet the railroad in Kansas.

For Texas's farmers, the railroads were a mixed blessing. They helped farmers expand their business by reaching more markets for their produce. But the railroads also charged high prices for freight to make the biggest possible profit at the farmers' expense. The situation became especially bad in the 1890s, when a period of drought plus a nationwide economic depression led to hard times for the farmers.

James S. Hogg, who was governor from 1891 to 1895, responded by creating the Texas Railroad Commission. The commission regulated rates and ensured fairer treatment for the farmers and ranchers who depended on the railroads. Jim Hogg was also

This photograph shows cowboys posing on and around a chuck wagon. Beans, corn bread or sourdough biscuits, and plenty of strong coffee were the staple foods on a cattle drive. Meals were supplemented with beef from the herd or game shot along the trail.

responsible for legislation aimed at helping ordinary Texans. Hogg's influence is still felt in Texas: In the words of a state historian, "Probably every governor since has been introduced by some master of ceremonies as 'the greatest governor since Jim Hogg.'"

Good Times and Bad

For Texas, the 20th century began with the worst natural disaster in American history. On the morning of September 8, 1900, a hurricane—a huge tropical storm—came roaring in from the Gulf of Mexico and flattened the city of Galveston. That night, 120-mile-per-hour winds pushed a wall of water fifteen feet high across the town. By the time the wind died down and the water swirled away, more than 5,000 people lay dead.

The problems of rebuilding the city led Galvestonians to reform their city government. Galveston adopted a new form of administration in which a commission of leading citizens, rather than the mayor and his political allies, took over essential public services. This Galveston Plan was later adopted by many other communities. Galveston's new government promptly built a seventeen-foot-high sea wall around the city to protect it from future storms.

Texas entered the 20th century with a population of more than 2.2 million—almost a fourfold increase

This photograph shows the devastation caused by the hurricane that wiped out Galveston in 1900. Thousands of people were killed on Galveston Island and more than 2,600 buildings were destroyed. Hundreds of charities and individuals across the country raised money and supplies to aid the survivors and help rebuild the city.

since 1870. Texas was mainly a rural state; only one in five Texans lived in a city or town at the turn of the century. The state had practically no industry. Most Texans made their living from the land, and more than half the state's farmers were tenant farmers—that is, they farmed on land owned by others and paid rent to the landowner.

Texas was in need of an economic boost. The first oil discovery in Texas took place in 1894 at Corsicana, in the north-central part of the state. At that time, however, there wasn't much of a market for oil. It wasn't until the coming of the automobile years later that petroleum (oil) products became a valuable commodity.

In January 1901, an event took place that helped transform Texas into an economic powerhouse. Drilling into the ground at a hill near the Gulf Coast town of Beaumont, Australian oilman Anthony Lucas made a startling discovery. A huge fountain of black liquid shot 200 feet into the air, the first of many Texas gushers. Lucas had tapped into a forty-acre lake of oil—a commodity as valuable as gold in those days—under Spindletop Hill.

The Lucas well produced 17 million barrels of oil in 1901, and by the end of the following year more than 100 other oil wells had been sunk around Spindletop. In the next years, giant corporations and lone profit seekers fanned out across Texas in search of oil. Many went broke; others made fantastic fortunes. The

first Texas oil boom was on. Prosperity from the oil boom, however, was not enough to keep problems at bay. The next decade brought new troubles to Texas at home, next door, and abroad.

James E. Ferguson, sometimes known as "Farmer Jim," became governor in 1914. Ferguson pledged to help the state's tenant farmers, few of whom had shared in the oil-boom prosperity. Ferguson proved a popular governor, and he was reelected in 1916. The following year, however, he angered Texans by cutting funding for the state university after a dispute with the school's leaders. Many citizens resented what they regarded as Ferguson's meddling in the university's affairs.

At the same time, the state legislature investigated Ferguson's financial records and discovered that he had received illegal campaign funds during the 1916 election. Ferguson was impeached—removed from office—and forbidden from holding office in Texas.

Meanwhile in 1910, a revolution toppled the Mexican government, beginning a decade of civil war. By 1915, Mexican revolutionaries, most notably Pancho Villa, were raiding

Jubilant oilmen stand beneath a successful well in this 1920 photograph (opposite). By 1925, more than eighty oil refineries were operating in Texas, and by the end of the decade Texas was the nation's leading oil-producing state.

American towns in the border states of Arizona, New Mexico, and Texas.

Once again relations between the United States and Mexico grew tense, and once again the American government sent troops to the Mexican border. Fortunately, war didn't break out as it had in 1846, but in 1917 an American force went into Mexico to chase Pancho Villa. The soldiers didn't catch Villa, but the expedition proved to be a valuable training exercise when the United States entered World War I a few months later. More than 200,000 Texans went to Europe to serve.

In the 1920s, cotton again became a major part of the state's economy. Mechanical harvesters made it easier to collect the crop, while improved irrigation techniques made cotton cultivation profitable even in the dry inland parts of the state. By the mid-1920s, Texas was exporting more than a million bales of cotton a year.

In 1925, Texans elected another Ferguson governor, Miriam Ferguson, wife of James E. Ferguson. Known as "Ma" Ferguson, she was only the second woman governor in American history. However, her critics charged—with some truth—that James Ferguson continued to run the state from his room in the governor's mansion.

New recruits line up for induction into the U.S. Army at Camp Travis, near San Antonio, in 1917. Camp Logan in Houston and Camp Bowie in Fort Worth were also major training centers during World War I.

The Depression and World War II

In 1930, a seventy-one-year-old oil-man named Columbus Marion Joiner arrived in East Texas. "Dad" Joiner was a wildcatter—an independent prospector who searches for new sources of oil.

On October 3, Joiner sunk a well about eight miles from the town of Henderson. If Joiner had drilled a thousand yards to the left or right, he would have hit rock or water—the dry hole that every wildcatter dreaded. Instead, Joiner brought in a gusher, and then another, a few miles to the north near Kilgore—and then yet another. Joiner had discovered the East Texas Oil Field, at 200 square miles the greatest oil deposit to be discovered in Texas—or anywhere else—up to that time. Within five years the field was producing 20,000 barrels a day; within a decade of the strike, the number rose to 200,000 barrels a day.

East Texas went from one of the state's poorest regions to a land of riches practically overnight. Property

West Texas was part of the Dust Bowl of the early 1930s, when years of drought dried up the soil and high winds carried it away. Many farm families, like the one in this photograph, left Texas in search of work in California and other states.

values shot skyward, enriching the farmers lucky enough to own land on the oil patch. Oil companies and investors rushed to East Texas with their checkbooks open. One business-man, the legendary H. L. Hunt, even-tually made $100 million from his 12,000-acre portion of the field.

For those Texans not fortunate enough to cash in on the oil strike, the 1930s was a decade of struggle. The nationwide economic depression that began with the stock market crash of 1929 brought much hardship to the state. By 1932, unemployment in Texas's towns and cities reached 250,000 people.

Most of the state's population still lived in rural areas, and these Texans were hit hard by a combination of the Depression, which sent crop prices into a steep decline, and natural disas-ters. Years of drought in the early 1930s brought ruin to many farms and ranches.

The state government struggled to cope with the Depression. Miriam Ferguson, elected to another term in 1933, established a state agency to provide help for the unemployed; her successor, James Allred, started a pen-sion program for the state's poorer older citizens. Texas also received much help from the federal New Deal programs introduced by President Franklin Roosevelt. Between 1933 and 1935, more than $50 million in federal aid flowed to Texas.

The state had several important friends in Washington during the 1930s, including John Nance Garner, vice president from 1933 to 1941, and Representative Sam Rayburn, soon to become Speaker of the House. Also up-and-coming was a young Texas congressman named Lyndon Johnson.

America's entry into World War II in 1941 brought Texas out of the Depression. Suddenly everything Texas produced—oil, cotton, beef, grain—was in great demand to meet the needs of the war effort. The war also brought major industry to Texas for the first time. Factories, especially aircraft plants, sprang up throughout the state. Shipyards in the Gulf Coast cities launched warships and cargo vessels as quickly as they could be built. The number of Texans working in industry tripled during the war years, and the value of the state's manufacturing quadrupled.

A grim cotton farmer (opposite) tries to find buyers for his crop in Weatherford in 1939. During the 1930s, cotton prices dropped to as low as 8 cents per pound. Some Texas towns sponsored "buy a bale" fund drives to keep local cotton farmers from going out of business.

Texas was a major center for pilot and aircrew training during World War II. In this photograph (above, right), Navy mechanics work on an engine at the Naval Air Training Center at Corpus Christi in 1942.

In another scene (right) from the Corpus Christi training center, student pilots await assignments for training flights.

The war turned Texas into a vast training camp as the military expanded posts like Fort Sam Houston at San Antonio and Fort Hood at Killeen and built many new ones. Altogether, 10 percent of the Americans who served in World War II—more than a million people—received their basic training in Texas.

Texas's human contribution to the war effort was no less important. The Texas men and women who served in the armed forces numbered close to 750,000. (Put another way, Texas in 1941 made up 5 percent of the nation's population, but Texans made up 7 percent of the armed forces.) More than 23,000 Texans gave their lives in the conflict.

Texans also reached the highest levels of command. Ovetta Culp Hobby,

Born in Denison in 1890, Dwight D. Eisenhower rose to supreme command of the Allied forces in Europe during World War II. In this photograph, the general talks with paratroopers about to take off for the D-Day landings in France in June 1944.

a Houston newspaper publisher, served as director of the WAACs (Woman's Auxiliary Army Corps). The state produced no fewer than 155 generals, and both the Allied supreme commander in Europe, General Dwight D. Eisenhower, and the commander-in-chief of the U.S. Pacific Fleet, Admiral Chester W. Nimitz, were native Texans. Just as famous was an enlisted man from Farmersville, Audie Murphy, who became the most highly decorated soldier of the war.

Into the Space Age

When peace came in August 1945, World War II had changed Texas even more profoundly than the cattle boom after the Civil War and the oil boom of the early 20th century. Texas was now a powerful industrial state. In the years ahead, Texas would become a major producer of aircraft, electrical equipment, and other products.

Texas's population stood at 5.8 million by the end of the 1940s, a jump of more than 1.5 million since 1930. For the first time, more Texans lived in towns and cities than in rural areas. During the war years and for decades afterward, many farmers—especially tenant farmers—left the land for jobs in Texas's growing cities.

The fastest-growing city was Houston. A quiet community of 300,000 people in 1930, Houston benefited greatly from the East Texas oil boom and from the industrial growth of the war years. Houston soon passed San Antonio to become Texas's largest city. Houston also became the second-largest port in the United States,

Texas past, Texas present: A 1945 photograph shows a cowboy watching as cattle graze almost in the shadows of Dallas's skyline. The post-World War II transformation of Texas from a rural to an urban state was one of the greatest changes in all of Texas's history.

thanks to the Houston Ship Channel, connecting the city to the Gulf of Mexico.

Oil remained the liveliest sector of Texas's economy in the years after World War II. By 1951, Texas's wells were pumping a staggering 1 billion barrels of oil each year. New oil deposits were discovered in Scurry County in 1949 and at Spraberry Field in West Texas in 1950. The Spraberry Field strike helped turn the small towns of Midland and Odessa into major oil centers.

It was offshore oil, however, that sparked Texas's greatest political controversy of the post-World War II years. Geologists believed that Texas's tidelands—the shallow coastal waters stretching into the Gulf of Mexico—were rich in oil. Naturally, Texas's politicians and businesspeople wanted to exploit this resource.

In 1947, however, the Supreme Court ruled that the federal government, not individual states, had control over tidelands. Texas challenged the court, but in 1950 the court again ruled against Texas.

Many Texans regarded the rulings as a grave economic loss. Thanks in large part to its oil wealth, the state traditionally kept its taxes low. Much of the funding for education and other public services came from leases of public land to oil companies, and royalties on oil pumped from that land. Texas politicians pointed out that the 1845 annexation agreement had given Texas ownership of the public lands within the state—and they argued that this agreement extended to the tidelands.

The controversy finally ended in 1953, shortly after Dwight Eisenhower took office as the first Texas-born president. Eisenhower signed a bill returning control of the tidelands to Texas.

The postwar years finally saw gains for the state's African Americans. Although African Americans made up almost a third of the state's people at the end of the Civil War, their percentage of the population had fallen steadily ever since as a result of black migration to the North. Those that remained in Texas endured poorly-funded schools, low-wage jobs or tenant farming, and segregation—the practice of separating African Americans from whites in education, public transportation, and housing. Lynchings and mob violence against African Americans were all too frequent in Texas, not just during Reconstruction but in the early part of the 20th century.

This pattern of discrimination also included Mexican Americans who were often denied the full rights of citizenship. But conditions for Texas's African and Mexican Americans improved in the 1940s and 1950s; the state's economic prosperity created better jobs, and the movement from the country to the cities began to break the pattern of rural poverty. In

In 1954 the Supreme Court ruled that public schools in the United States could not be separated by race. Throughout the South, there was resistance to the ruling. In this 1956 photograph (right), a state ranger talks to white students while on duty at Mansfield Texas High School. A cloth dummy has been hung above the entrance to the school.

This aerial view (below) shows "rocket park" on the grounds of Houston's Johnson Space Center. Opened in 1961, the complex employed more than 5,000 people by the end of the 1960s.

The space center's greatest triumph came in July 1969, when astronaut Neil Armstrong became the first human to set foot on the moon (below, right). Armstrong's words when the space capsule touched down on the moon—"Houston . . . Tranquillity base here. The Eagle has landed!"—were heard by millions around the world.

the 1950s and 1960s, Supreme Court rulings and federal civil rights laws ensured blacks and Hispanics political rights and outlawed segregation in education and other areas. Some white Texans were angered by what they saw as federal "interference" in Texas's affairs. Still, Texas escaped the violence and bitterness that marked desegregation in the other states in the South.

At the same time, Texas began to play a major role in the technological revolution sweeping the postwar world. In 1959, Jack Kilby, an engineer for the Texas Instruments Corporation, developed the integrated circuit—the microchip that is now at the heart of machines from personal computers to cars and robots. And in 1963, President John F. Kennedy announced Houston as the site for NASA's $760-million Manned Spacecraft Center, the new headquarters for the nation's space program. Kennedy's decision was influenced by his Texan vice president, Lyndon Baines Johnson.

On November 22, 1963, Kennedy and Johnson arrived in Dallas for a visit. While driving through the city, bullets from an assassin's rifle killed the president and seriously wounded Texas governor John Connally. Two days later, Dallas nightclub owner Jack Ruby shot and killed the assassin, Lee Harvey Oswald, in the Dallas jail. The tragedy of those three days in Dallas still lingers.

In this photograph, Lee Harvey Oswald is shown being arrested hours after the murder of President John F. Kennedy. In addition to killing the president and wounding Texas governor John Connally, Oswald shot and killed a Dallas policeman, J. D. Tippitt, before his capture.

Changing Times

Lyndon Johnson was sworn in as president less than two hours after Kennedy's death. The following year, Johnson was elected president in his own right with a landslide victory in the election of 1964.

Born on a farm near the Perdenales River in 1908, "LBJ" was a product of the rough-and-tumble world of Texas politics. In his years in Congress, first as a representative and then as a senator and senate majority leader, Johnson earned a reputation as a man who could get things done.

As president, Johnson used his political know-how to win passage of major legislation like the Civil Rights

Standing next to a tearful Jacqueline Kennedy, the president's widow, Lyndon Baines Johnson takes the oath of office as president shortly after John F. Kennedy's death. One Texas historian described the ambitious, energetic, and sometimes ruthless LBJ as "the Texas mystique personified."

Act of 1964. But Johnson's presidency was overshadowed by America's involvement in the Vietnam War. In 1968, worn out by the strain of the controversial conflict, Johnson surprised the nation by announcing he would not run for another term. He returned to Texas and spent his last years in retirement on his ranch.

The 1970s was another prosperous time for Texas—once again thanks to oil. The price of oil shot up during the early 1970s, and so did Texas's economy. Money from oil fueled a boom in real estate and banking and helped other industries thrive as well.

The state's population jumped from just over 11 million in 1970 to more than 14 million a decade later—an increase of more than 27 percent. Part of this increase came from a wave of newcomers drawn by job opportunities as companies left the "rust belt" states of the North and Midwest for the "sun belt" states of the Southwest.

While Texas's economy went into high gear, the state's politics underwent great changes. Texas had traditionally voted Democratic, but the Republican party gained a strong foothold in the state starting in the 1960s. In 1978, Republican William P. Clements, Jr., became the first Republican in the governor's mansion since the days of Reconstruction. Other prominent Texas Republicans included John Tower, a U.S. senator from 1961 to 1985, and former governor John Connally, who switched from the Democratic party and served as secretary of the treasury in President Richard Nixon's cabinet.

The 1970s also brought Texas's Mexican-American and African-American communities a greater share of political power. Houston lawyer Barbara Jordan was elected to the House of Representatives in 1973—the first African-American woman from a former Confederate state to serve in Congress. Mickey Leland, elected to the House in 1978, chaired the Congressional Black Caucus—an association of African-American representatives—before his death in a plane crash in 1989.

Despite Texas's strong Mexican heritage, only about 100,000 people of Mexican birth or ancestry lived in Texas in 1900. In the first decades of the century, however, hundreds of thousands of Mexicans fled political and economic chaos in their homeland and settled in Texas. By 1950, 1.5 million Mexican Americans lived in Texas; by the 1970s, nearly one in four Texans was of Mexican ancestry.

Texas offered more opportunities than Mexico, but life for Mexican immigrants and their descendants was often hard. Many worked at low-paying

jobs in agriculture or industry; language was often a barrier to better jobs and education. Organizations like La Raza Unidá (United Race), founded in Crystal City by José and Luiz Gutiérrez in 1970, formed to improve conditions for Mexican Americans in Texas and other states.

At the same time, growing numbers of Texas's Mexican Americans became successful in government and business. Henry Gonzalez of San Antonio was first elected to the House of Representatives in 1961; he was joined in 1965 by Kika de la Garza, who served as chairman of the House Agricultural Committee. And in 1981, thirty-four-year-old Henry Cisneros was elected mayor of San Antonio—the first Hispanic mayor of a major American city.

Barbara Jordan's political career began in 1966, when she became the first African American to win election to Texas's state senate in almost a century. Jordan (opposite) has been active as a writer and educator since her retirement from Congress in 1979.

Texas's Chicanos—as Americans of Mexican ancestry are sometimes called—organized to seek a greater share of the state's political life in the 1960s and 1970s. This mural (above, right) in South El Paso displays the thunderbird to proclaim pride in La Raza Unidá.

By 1981, more than a thousand Hispanics held political office in Texas. Among them was Henry Cisneros (right), the first Mexican-American mayor of San Antonio since Juan Seguín in the 1840s. Cisneros was appointed secretary of housing and urban development by President Clinton in 1993.

Texas Faces the Future

Texas rolled into the 1980s on a tide of oil wealth. In the first years of the decade, however, the price of oil took a nosedive, dropping from $30 a barrel in the late 1970s to $14 in 1985.

For Texas, the result of the "oil bust" was the worst economic crisis since the Depression of the 1930s. Because so much of the state's economy depended on oil, the impact of falling prices went far beyond the oil industry itself. Construction of new buildings came to a halt. Banks that had loaned money freely for years now found themselves with few funds. The gleaming office towers of Houston and Dallas were full of empty floors.

Unemployment rates shot up as oil prices went down. In 1985, Texas's jobless rate rose higher than the national average for the first time in nearly twenty years.

Because it depended on oil taxes for one third of its income, the state government also suffered. After the oil bust, tax revenues from oil dropped to about 10 percent. In 1987, the state legislature passed a tax increase of almost $6 billion dollars to help make up the shortfall. It was a controversial action, given the state's long history of low taxes.

By 1987, Texas's economy began to pick up, although the national

BIENVENIDOS A MEXICO

recession of the late 1980s and early 1990s slowed down this recovery. To revive local economies, many Texas communities worked together to convince out-of-state companies to "come on down" to Texas. In one well-known case, the retail store chain J. C. Penney was persuaded to relocate its headquarters to Plano, bringing 4,000 much needed jobs to the area.

In recent years, Texas's economy has become much more diverse. Today, service industries account for more than half of the state's wealth. The growth in manufacturing that began in World War II has continued—for example, Texas is now the nation's second-largest manufacturer of aircraft.

Houston's expansion since World War II has been remarkable. The city's population grew by more than a million people between 1950 and the early 1980s, when the "oil bust" slowed its growth. Houston (opposite) is now not only the largest city in Texas but the fourth-largest city in the United States.

Tourists return to Texas from a shopping trip south of the border (above). Economic ties between Mexican and American communities in the Rio Grande Valley are close and growing, but illegal immigration into Texas remains a major concern.

While Texas struggled out of the oil bust in the 1980s, Mexico's economy went into a deep slump. As a result, illegal immigration increased as hard-pressed Mexicans crossed into Texas and other border states in search of work. Texas's long boundary with

Mexico—and the fact that many South Texas towns have Mexican sister cities just across the border—makes it difficult for the U.S. Border Patrol to keep out illegal immigrants.

In South Texas, however, ties with Mexico are close, and illegal immigrants often play a large role in the local economy. "The Mexicans are taking jobs that no one here is taking," said a professor from the University of Texas in 1993, responding to a much-publicized crackdown on illegal immigration between El Paso and Ciudad Juarez on the Mexican side of the Rio Grande. People on both sides of the border hoped that the 1994 passage of the North American Free Trade Agreement (NAFTA) would ease the immigration problem by strengthening Mexico's economy.

Texas began the 1990s with a population of nearly 17 million—only California and New York have more people. The state's population grew by almost 20 percent in the 1980s—a lower rate than during the boom years of the 1970s, but still twice the national average. Today, four out of five Texans live in a town or city, and close to half of the state's citizens live in two urban areas—Dallas-Fort Worth and the Houston-Galveston metropolitan areas.

In recent years Texans have been prominent on the national political scene. Born in Massachusetts but a Texan since the late 1940s, George Bush served as vice president (1981–89) and president (1989–93). Billionaire businessman H. Ross Perot, born in Texarkana, caused a political sensation when he ran as an independent candidate for the White House in the election of 1992. Former senator Lloyd Bentsen, an unsuccessful candidate for the vice presidency in 1988, was named secretary of the treasury in 1993. After eight years as mayor of San Antonio, Henry Cisneros also became a member of President Bill Clinton's cabinet as secretary of housing and urban development.

Some call the 1990s "the decade of the woman" in Texas politics, because so many women were elected to public offices. Former state treasurer Ann Richards was elected governor in 1990, and another former treasurer, Kay Bailey Hutchison, won election to the U.S. Senate in 1993.

Author John Steinbeck once described Texas as not just a state, but a state of mind. Texans have long been famous worldwide for the fierce pride they take in their state—a pride based not just on the state's size, but also on its long and unique history. As Texas approaches the 21st century, that pride will sustain the state's people as they work to meet the challenges of the future.

With her election to state treasurer in 1982, Ann Richards (right) became the first woman to hold state office in Texas since "Ma" Ferguson in the 1930s. After winning the governor's race in 1990, Richards was nicknamed "Action Annie" by Texas journalists for her vigorous approach to government.

For all its urbanization, Texas remains a state of wide-open spaces and great natural beauty. In this photograph, a lone car passes a magnificent rock formation in Big Bend National Park.

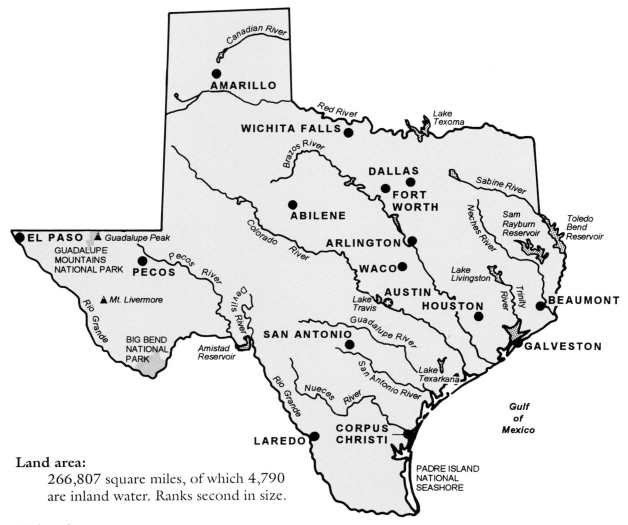

Land area:
    266,807 square miles, of which 4,790 are inland water. Ranks second in size.

Major rivers:
    The Brazos; the Canadian; the Colorado; the Devils; the Guadalupe; the Neches; the Nueces; the Pecos; the Red; the Rio Grande; the San Antonio; the Sabine; the Trinity.

Highest point: Guadalupe Peak, 8,751 ft.

Major bodies of water:
    The Amistad Reservoir; the Sam Rayburn Reservoir; Lake Livingston; Lake Texarkana; Lake Texoma; Lake Travis; Toledo Bend Reservoir. Many created artificially for irrigation or as reservoirs.

Population: 17,655,650 (1992)
Rank: 3rd
    1900: 3,048,710
    1850: 212,592

Population of major cities (1990):

Houston	1,630,864
Dallas	1,007,618
San Antonio	935,933
El Paso	515,342
Austin	465,622
Fort Worth	447,619
Arlington	261,721

Ethnic breakdown by percentage (1990):

White	60.5%
African American	11.6%
Hispanic	25.5%
Asian/Pacific Islander	1.8%
Native American	0.3%
Other	0.1%

Climate:
    Average January temperature: 46°F
    Average July temperature: 84°F
    Climate varies widely.

Economy:
    Manufacturing (oil refining, heavy machinery, transportation equipment, computers and electronic equipment, chemicals, and textiles); agriculture (cotton, sorghum, wheat, corn, citrus fruits, and nuts); beef cattle and hogs; oil and natural gas; and tourism.

State government:
    Legislature: 31-member Senate and 150-member House of Representatives. Senators serve 4-year terms, representatives 2-year terms.
    Governor: Serves a 4-year term. Cabinet members and three members of the Texas Railroad Commission are popularly elected, not appointed.
    Courts: The Supreme Court, divided into 14 districts, is Texas's highest court. There are many district, county, and municipal courts.
State capital: Austin

State Flag

Adopted by the Republic of Texas in 1839, Texas's state flag consists of a single white star on a blue field and one stripe each of red and white. Each color represents a virtue: White stands for strength, red for courage, and blue for loyalty.

State Seal

The state seal features a lone star enclosed in a wreath, with the words "The State of Texas" appearing around the border. The base color is gold.

State Motto

The simple state motto, "Friendship," has its origin in *Tejas*, which means "land of friends" or "allies" in the language of a Native American group, the Caddos.

State Nickname

"The Lone Star State."

Places

The Alamo, San Antonio

Amon Carter Museum of Western Art, Fort Worth

Aransas National Wildlife Refuge, Rockport

Big Bend National Park, Boerne

Border Patrol Museum, El Paso

Caddoan Mounds Historic Site, Alto

Cattlemen's Museum, Fort Worth

Chamizal National Memorial, El Paso

Dallas Arboretum and Botanical Garden, Dallas

Dallas Museum of African-American Life, Dallas

Dinosaur Valley State Park, Glen Rose

Eisenhower Birthplace National Park, Denison

El Paso Museum of History, El Paso

Fighting Air Command National Museum, Denton

Fort Concho, San Angelo

Fort Worth Museum of Science and Industry, Fort Worth

Guadalupe Mountains National Park, Salt Flat

Hall of State, Dallas

Institute of Texan Cultures, San Antonio

John F. Kennedy Memorials and Assassination Museum, Dallas

Kimball Art Museum, Fort Worth

to See

Lyndon B. Johnson Space Center, Houston

Matagorda Island State Park, Port O'Connor

Museum of Oriental Cultures, Corpus Christi

Old Fort Davis National Historical Site, Alpine

Old Stone Fort, Nagadoches

Padre Island National Seashore, Padre Island

Pioneer Memorial Museum, Fredericksburg

River Walk, San Antonio

Sam Houston Memorial Museum, Huntsville

San Jose Mission, San Antonio

Santa Anna National Wildlife Refuge, Alamo

Six Flags Over Texas (theme park), Arlington

Spindletop Museum, Beaumont

Star of the Republic Museum, Washington

State Capitol building, Austin

State Fair Park and Museums, Houston

State Library and Archives Building, Austin

Texas Memorial Museum, Austin

Texas Ranger Museum, Waco

USS *Texas*/ San Jacinto Battleground State Park, Houston

State Flower

Texas's state flower is the bluebonnet. According to an Indian legend, a young girl tried to end a drought by burning her favorite doll as a sacrifice. When the rain came, a bluebonnet rose from the place where the doll's ashes had fallen.

State Bird

The northern species of mockingbird is Texas's state bird. A small gray-and-white bird with a long tail, it's called a mockingbird because it imitates the songs and calls of other birds.

State Tree

Texas's state tree is the pecan, a member of the walnut family. Tall and fast-growing, the tree produces a rich, flavorful nut often used in pies, candy, and other foods.

Texas History

c. 1500 Caddo Confederacy becomes dominant Native American group in Texas

1528–41 Cabeza de Vaca and Francisco de Coronado explore Texas

1682 The first Spanish settlement is founded near present-day El Paso

1685 Fort St. Louis is established on Matagorda Bay

1690 Spain founds first Texas mission

1691 Texas officially comes under Spanish rule

1718 The Alamo is built at present-day San Antonio

1821 Mexico gains independence; Stephen Austin brings American settlers to Texas

1836 Texas declares independence; Texan forces are defeated at the Alamo and Goliad but are victorious at San Jacinto; Texas becomes an independent nation

1837 The Lone Star Republic wins recognition from the United States

1845 Texas becomes twenty-eighth state

1846–48 Mexican War; Mexico gives up claims to Texas after U.S. victory

1850 Compromise of 1850 establishes Texas's borders

1861 Texas secedes from Union and joins Confederacy

1865 Last Civil War battle fought at Palmitto Ranch, Texas

American

1492 Christopher Columbus reaches the New World

1607 Jamestown (Virginia) founded by English colonists

1620 *Mayflower* arrives at Plymouth (Massachusetts)

1754–63 French and Indian War

1765 Parliament passes Stamp Act

1775–83 Revolutionary War

1776 Signing of the Declaration of Independence

1788–90 First congressional elections

1791 Bill of Rights added to U.S. Constitution

1803 Louisiana Purchase

1812–14 War of 1812

1820 Missouri Compromise

1836 Battle of the Alamo, Texas

1846–48 Mexican War

1849 California Gold Rush

1860 South Carolina secedes from Union

1861–65 Civil War

1862 Lincoln signs Homestead Act

1863 Emancipation Proclamation

1865 President Lincoln assassinated (April 14)

1865–77 Reconstruction in the South

1866 Civil Rights bill passed

1881 President James Garfield shot (July 2)

History

1896 First Ford automobile is made

1898–99 Spanish-American War

1901 President William McKinley is shot (Sept. 6)

1917 U.S. enters World War I

1922 Nineteenth Amendment passed, giving women the vote

1929 U.S. stock market crash; Great Depression begins

1933 Franklin D. Roosevelt becomes president; begins New Deal

1941 Japanese attack Pearl Harbor (Dec. 7); U.S. enters World War II

1945 U.S. drops atomic bomb on Hiroshima and Nagasaki; Japan surrenders, ending World War II

1963 President Kennedy assassinated (November 22)

1964 Civil Rights Act passed

1965–73 Vietnam War

1968 Martin Luther King, Jr., shot in Memphis (April 4)

1974 President Richard Nixon resigns because of Watergate scandal

1979–81 Hostage crisis in Iran: 52 Americans held captive for 444 days

1989 End of U.S.-Soviet cold war

1991 Gulf War

1993 U.S. signs North American Free Trade Agreement with Canada and Mexico

Texas History

1866–67 First cattle drives bring longhorns from Texas

1870 Texas rejoins the Union

1876 State constitution adopted

1888 Capitol building at Austin is completed

1900 Hurricane devastates Galveston

1901 Texas oil boom begins

1916–17 Border clashes in Texas lead to conflict between U.S. and Mexico

1930 Exploitation of East Texas Oil Field begins

1953 U.S. government relinquishes control of the oil-rich Texas tidelands

1962 NASA's Manned Space Center opens in Houston

1963 President John F. Kennedy is assassinated in Dallas; Texan Lyndon B. Johnson becomes president of U.S.

1966 Texas abolishes poll tax in an advance for civil rights

1973 Barbara Jordan is the first African-American woman elected to Congress from the South

1983 Drop in oil prices leads to economic slump throughout Texas

1988 State government declares drought disaster

1993 U.S. government cancels Waxahatchie Supercollider project

Stephen Austin (1793–1836)
Son of **Moses Austin (1761–1821)**, Stephen Austin led the first large group of Americans to settle in Texas. Active in the fight for Texan independence, he served as the Republic of Texas's first secretary of state.

Sam Houston (1793–1863)
Commander of the Texan forces at San Jacinto, Houston became the Republic of Texas's first president and, after annexation, one of its first U.S. senators. Elected governor in 1859, he was forced from office because he opposed Texas's secession.

Jose Antonio Navarro (1795–1871) One of the founders of the Republic of Texas, Navarro was born in San Antonio. He helped draft

Quanah Parker

Texas's Declaration of Independence and, later, the state constitution.

Elisabet Ney (1833–1907)
This German-born sculptor helped found the Texas Fine Arts Association and was active in the struggle for women's rights.

Quanah Parker (1845–1911)
Son of a Comanche chief and a white woman, Parker led his band in resisting white settlement. After being forced onto a reservation in 1875, Parker became a successful businessman and land agent, making deals with white investors that benefited his tribe.

Scott Joplin (1868–1917)
Born and raised in Texarkana, Joplin was the first major African-American composer. His music ranges from ragtime songs to opera.

John Nance Garner (1868–1967) "Cactus Jack" Garner grew up in Red River County. A Democrat, he served in the House of Representatives for thirty years, including a term as speaker, and was Franklin Roosevelt's vice president from 1933 to 1941.

Miriam A. Ferguson (1875–1961) Wife of **Governor James E. Ferguson (1871–1944)**, "Ma" Ferguson was elected governor in 1924 following her husband's removal from office. She served until 1935.

Arthur ("Jack") Johnson (1878–1946) In 1908, Galveston-born Jack Johnson became the first African-American boxer to win the world heavyweight title.

Sam Rayburn (1882–1961)
"Mr. Sam" spent nearly fifty years representing Texas in Congress, including seventeen years as Speaker of the House of Representatives.

Chester Nimitz (1885–1966)
Born in Fredericksburg, Nimitz graduated from the U.S. Naval Academy in 1905. Commander of the U.S. Pacific Fleet in World War II, Nimitz scored several remarkable victories over Japan. He served as chief of naval operations after the war.

Dwight D. Eisenhower (1890–1969) A native of Denison, Eisenhower was Allied supreme commander in Europe during World War II.

He became the first Texas-born president in 1952.

Katharine Anne Porter (1890–1980) This journalist, novelist, and short-story writer was born in Indian Creek. Her *Collected Stories* won the 1966 Pulitzer Prize for literature.

Howard Hughes (1905–76) After inheriting the Houston-based Hughes Tool Company, this legendary financier became a movie producer, aircraft designer, pilot, and finally a club and casino owner in Las Vegas.

Oveta Culp Hobby (b. 1905) A Killeen native, Hobby organized the Women's Auxiliary Army Corps (the WAACs) during World War II and served as secretary of health, education, and welfare (1953–55).

Lyndon Baines Johnson (1908–72) Born near Johnson City, "LBJ" was elected vice president in 1960 and became president following John F. Kennedy's assassination in Dallas in 1963. He was elected president in his own right in 1964.

Henry B. Gonzalez (b. 1916) The first Texan of Mexican heritage to win election to Congress, Gonzalez has served in the House of Representatives since 1961. He is a native of San Antonio.

John B. Connally (1917–93) Governor of Texas from 1963 to 1969, Connally was severely wounded during the assassination of John F. Kennedy.

George Bush (b. 1924) Bush moved to Texas and entered the oil business in 1948. Elected to Congress in 1966, he also served as CIA director and became Ronald Reagan's vice president in 1980. He became the nation's forty-first president in 1988, but was defeated in the 1992 election.

Tom Landry (b. 1924) A football legend, Mission-born Landry was head coach of the Dallas Cowboys from 1960 to 1989, leading the Cowboys to five Super Bowl appearances and two victories.

Alvin Ailey (1931–89) A native of Rogers, Ailey founded the Alvin Ailey City Center for Dance Theater in 1958. His dance troupe has toured across six continents and won international recognition for its vibrant, inspiring performances.

Buddy Holly

Buddy Holly (1936–59) One of the most original of the early rock 'n' rollers, this Lubbock native's career was cut short by a fatal plane crash. His songs influenced later pop music.

Barbara Jordan (b. 1936) Born in Houston, Jordan was a state senator and civil rights adviser to President Johnson before her election to the House of Representatives in 1972. She served until 1979.

Henry G. Cisneros (b. 1947) The first Hispanic mayor of a major American city, Cisneros served four terms as mayor of San Antonio. He is currently serving as secretary of housing and urban development in the Clinton administration.

Pictures in this volume:

Daughters of the Republic of Texas Library: 18

Friends of the Governor's Mansion: 16

Gillespie County Historical Society: 22

Governor's Office: 53 (top)

Greater Houston Partnership: 50

Housing and Urban Development: 49 (bottom)

Library of Congress: 9 (bottom), 13, 14, 19, 21, 24 (bottom), 25, 27 (bottom), 28, 29, 30, 32, 33, 34, 37, 40, 42, 43, 45, 46, 47, 48, 60, 61

NASA: 45

National Academy of Design: 24 (top)

National Archives: 38, 39, 41 (both), 49 (top)

National Park Service: 11

National Museum of Art: 12, 27 (top)

San Antonio Missions Historical Park: 7

Texas Department Travel: 2, 51, 53

Texas State Library, Archives Division: 17, 35, 44

The Witte Museum, San Antonio: 9 (top)

About the author:

Charles A. Wills is a writer, editor, and consultant specializing in American history. He has written, edited, or contributed to more than thirty books, including many volumes in The Millbrook Press's *American Albums from the Collections of the Library of Congress* and *State Historical Albums* series. Wills lives in Dutchess County, New York.

Suggested reading:

Carpenter, Allan. *The New Enchantment of America: Texas.* Chicago: Childrens Press, 1978.

Fehrenbach, T.R. *Lone Star: A History of Texas and Texans.* New York: American Legacy Press.

Fisher, Leonard Everett. *The Alamo.* New York: Holiday House, 1987.

Frantz, Joe. *Texas: A Bicentennial History.* New York: Norton, 1976.

Michener, James. *The Eagle and the Raven.* Austin, TX: State House Press, 1990.

Richardson, Rupert. *Texas, the Lone Star State.* Englewood Cliffs, NJ: Prentiss Hall, 1988.

Stein, R. Conrad. *America the Beautiful: Texas.* Chicago: Childrens Press, 1989.

For more information contact:

Texas Department of Commerce
Tourism Division
PO Box 12728
Austin, TX 78711
(512) 462-9191

Texas State Library and Archives
PO Box 1297
Austin, TX 78711
(512) 463-5480

INDEX

Page numbers in *italics* indicate illustrations